END AND BEGINNING

ALSO BY JOHN MASEFIELD

PLAYS:

THE FAITHFUL: *A Tragedy in Three Acts*
GOOD FRIDAY: *A Play in Verse*
ESTHER. (*Adapted and partially translated from the French of Jean Racine,*
BERENICE. (*Adapted from the French of Jean Racine*)
MELLONEY HOLTSPUR; or, The Pangs of Love. *A Play in Four Acts*
A KING'S DAUGHTER: *A Tragedy in Verse in Four Acts*
THE TRIAL OF JESUS
THE TRAGEDY OF NAN
TRISTAN AND ISOLT: *A Play in Verse*
THE COMING OF CHRIST: *A New Hymn of the Resurrection written in Play form*
EASTER: *A Play for Singers*
END AND BEGINNING

POETRY:

DAUBER
THE DAFFODIL FIELDS
PHILIP THE KING AND OTHER POEMS
LOLLINGDON DOWNS AND OTHER POEMS, WITH SONNETS
A POEM AND TWO PLAYS (*Rosas, a poem; The Locked Chest; The Sweeps of Ninety-Eight*)
REYNARD THE FOX
ENSLAVED AND OTHER POEMS
RIGHT ROYAL
SELECTED POEMS
KING COLE AND OTHER POEMS
COLLECTED POEMS
MIDSUMMER NIGHT AND OTHER TALES IN VERSE
MINNIE MAYLOW'S STORY AND OTHER TALES AND SCENES
A TALE OF TROY

FICTION:

SARD HARKER
ODTAA
THE MIDNIGHT FOLK
THE HAWBUCKS

GENERAL:

GALLIPOLI
THE OLD FRONT LINE
ST. GEORGE AND THE DRAGON
THE BATTLE OF THE SOMME
RECENT PROSE
WITH THE LIVING VOICE
THE "WANDERER" OF LIVERPOOL
POETRY: A Lecture

END AND BEGINNING

BY

JOHN MASEFIELD

★

NEW YORK
THE MACMILLAN COMPANY
1933

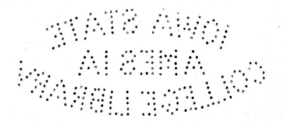
PRINTED IN THE UNITED STATES OF AMERICA
BY THE POLYGRAPHIC COMPANY OF AMERICA, N.Y.

To
FLORENCE

END AND BEGINNING

PERSONS

MARY STUART	SYBIL M. HERIZ-SMITH
FIRST WOMAN	JUDITH MASEFIELD
SECOND WOMAN	ROSE BRUFORD
AN OFFICER	LESLIE DAVEY
A NOBLE	ALBERT FOWLER
A SPIRIT OF BEAUTY	CHRYSTABEL DALE ROBERTS

The scene is a small room in Fotheringhay Castle. A settle with a canopy is in the centre. A small table with ink, pens, wine and a cup is to the Actors' Left of this settle.

END AND BEGINNING

I am that Mary Stuart, the Queen of Scotland:
Once Queen of France, now prisoner here in England.

      *   *   *

Evil indeed were my days as the Scottish Queen.

      *   *   *

When Bothwell and others murdered my husband,
    Darnley,
Bothwell seized me as prize, for he meant to be King.
His fellow-murderers hunted him out of Scotland
And shut me up in Lochleven and seized my realm.

For one brief hour I was free:
Men who were loyal came to me:
For one brief hour, I hoped, in vain,
To win my son and throne again.

I was betrayed again when the battle was joined.
I had to ride for life, drinking the burns
And sleeping in the heather like the grouse.

So, since Scotland was lost, without hope thence-
    forward,

END AND BEGINNING

I came to England to ask for help from the Queen
Who shut me in prison straight and has kept me
    prisoned
These nineteen years, nearly a half of my life.

It has been strictest prison: in all those years
I have been watched and guarded, my people
    searched.
Such was my past.

*   *   *

Last June, my enemies contrived my ruin.
Their agents stirred some hotheads to conspire
To league the French and Spanish against England
And set me free. These hotheads wrote to me.
I sent such answer as a Queen might send.

*   *   *

My answer was in cipher. It was taken
By English spies, who soon deciphered it,
And wrote what they declared a copy of it,
But to it added what their hatred urged,
Passages about killing of the Queen.

Then, being satisfied, they seized the plotters
(Men whom their agents only had set on)
Tortured them to confessing anything,
Then barbarously killed them publicly.
All this in the design to have me killed.

END AND BEGINNING

When they were ready, they proclaimed abroad
How God in His great Mercy had revealed
A hellish practice of the Scottish Queen
Against the life of Queen Elizabeth;
How murderers had sworn to run her through
And how French armies and the Spanish fleet
Were coming, to cut every English throat
And make me Queen of England and of Scotland.

The church-bells rang, by order, in each parish
For joy that such a plot had been frustrated.

When they had poisoned every English heart
Against me, to the full, they sent the Peers
All the great nobles of the Kingdom, led
By Burghley, my chief enemy, "to try me."
That was the phrase they used: they meant my death.

I, an anointed Queen, unjustly prisoned,
Was threatened, and brow-beaten and accused.
The evidence was their own forgeries
And madness from the tortured men now dead;
Nothing of mine was brought, nor could be brought.
No letter, not one word, written or spoken.
But since they meant my death, I was condemned
To suffer death.
                    I stand here under sentence.
Certain not to receive more mercy now
Than in the past: certain not to be rescued:
Certain to die in very few more days.
I try not to dread death; but oh I dread

END AND BEGINNING

Lest murderers should kill me secretly
Then publish that I killed myself, defiling
This that God consecrated to be Queen.
I pray I be not murdered secretly.

Such is my present: for my future, this
My life's device: the puzzle "In my End
Is my Beginning": I have often wondered
And wonder now, what future it foretells.

Rescue and freedom and the hope of life
These I put by: they cannot come to me.
I will endure whatever God shall send
And bear His gift of being Queen unshaken
While He gives breath to me.

        For not much longer
Shall I have breath. The winter night is dark.
I will pray God, and then lie down to rest.
        (She goes Left Back)
        (The WOMEN ENTER *on lower stage,* FIRST
        WOMAN *Left,* SECOND *Right. They go up on
        to the upper stage and stand Centre.)*

FIRST WOMAN

A man in a black cloak hastens down
The palace stairs in a sleeping town

A white-faced man who means no good
With a parchment, sealed, hid under his hood

END AND BEGINNING

He mounts his horse and he rides north west
He rides like Death and he looks unblest.

Is it a head or a skull that hides
Under his cloak as he rides and rides.

He is a man, for he draws quick breath
But he rides like Death and he brings death

Spirits like his go by in glare
When the hounds of hell are in the air.

SECOND WOMAN

Another man rides the self-same course
Through the sleeping land on a Queen's horse,

A gallows-tree man, whose fit salute
Is the fox's howl and the owl's hoot.

He sings, as he rides, an evil strain,
He looks like Cain and he is Cain.

What does he bear in the canvas pack
Buckled against him on his back?

When he stops to drink, he draws it bare:—
An axe-blade bright as a plough's share.

He kisses the blade and cries, "My chink,
You shall soon eat: you shall soon drink."

END AND BEGINNING

The riders have met: they ride like friends
Who have ends in common and evil ends.

They turn at the cross: they draw nigh
They are coming here, not going by.

The horn at the castle gate is blown
The gate opens, the hinges groan.

They ride within to the castle-yard
The gate shuts, it is locked and barred.

There are lights in the yard: the gaoler goes
To ask 'Who has come there?' Now he knows.
                    (*Indicating Right Back*)
And now they enter the gaoler's den.
Lighten our Night from midnight men.

SECOND WOMAN

What do they plot in the gaoler's room
Whispering white-faced in the gloom?

No great good from a secret three:—
Verjuice, vigilance, gallows-tree.

What do they whisper? Why do they call
For a wooden stage in the castle hall?

6

END AND BEGINNING

Why does vigilance creep the stair
Up, up, up, to the curtain there?

Why does he stand there, breathing deep
Near midnight thus, with the Queen asleep?

Why has he come here? What does he mean?
        (OFFICER ENTERS. *Right Back*)

OFFICER

Women. I want to see the Queen.

FIRST WOMAN

The Queen, our lady, has gone to rest.

OFFICER

Go, then, and rouse her: it were best.

FIRST WOMAN

Sir, we are loath to break her sleep.

OFFICER

The news I bring her will not keep.

END AND BEGINNING

FIRST WOMAN

Sir, may we know what news you bring?

OFFICER

Fetch me this Queen to know the thing.

FIRST WOMAN

Sir, may we know what noble calls?

OFFICER

One who has stages built in halls
And hung with black, for what may chance.
One with men masked as for a dance
Also in black, a sullen two.
Sharp practice is the craft they do.
One who has passports that shall free
All prisoners whatsoe'er they be.
Yellow-sealed passports writ in red
Go: fetch your lady out of bed.

FIRST WOMAN

Since you bring freedom, I will go.

(FIRST WOMAN *goes*)

8

END AND BEGINNING

(OFFICER, *indicating throne*)

You, pretty mistress, may I know
What this gay trumpery may be?

SECOND WOMAN

Our lady's, the Queen's, dignity.

OFFICER

Our dignity? the Queen's? Her state?
Her throne shall rest me as I wait. (*He sits*)

SECOND WOMAN

You must not sit in the Queen's chair.

OFFICER

Must not, my mistress? I am there.

SECOND WOMAN

You shall not do her this offence.

9

END AND BEGINNING

Girl, do you think to drive me hence?
You and your sisters and this Queen
That memory of what once has been?
I do my will here, nor think twice
Of this old dignity's device
But beat it down where it belongs.
                    (*He tears down the device*)

SECOND WOMAN

They shall not let you do these wrongs,
I'll call her men. (*She goes Left Back*)

OFFICER

                    Call whom you will.
Now all the castle is as still
As the deep grave: but silently
My carpenters all work for me
Raising a stage within the hall,
Making no hammer-noise at all,
As men who fashion coffins use.
All silent fastening with screws.
And some strew black and others red
Where this, the Scottish Queen, shall tread

Down in the barns, the halberdiers
Sleep with the straw about their ears.

END AND BEGINNING

Among the ashes crickets keep
Their cry to folk who cannot sleep.
The owls hoot and the foxes bark;
The sick man's candle shocks the dark;
All the invisible great Night
Heaves slowly over bringing light.

And when the light comes, then, ah then,
Word will go thrilling among men.
When cricket, owl and fox are gone
Men will come thronging, and anon
When all the gateways gleam with spears
And the slow death-bell nulls the ears
And all the hundreds in the hall
Wait for a woman's step and all
Turn at her coming and a bright
Steel axeblade flashes in the light . . .
But the deer comes: the hunt is up.

> (MARY ENTERS, *Left Back. She comes down the
> stage to the Centre. The two* WOMEN *keep well
> back to the Left of the stage.* MARY *expects the
> visitor to be a murderer sent to kill her.*)

OFFICER

Madam, I have a word for you. Attend.
You, madam, were admonished to repent
And to confess your manifold offences
Against Elizabeth our gracious Queen.
You have not shewn contrition nor sense of fault

END AND BEGINNING

Therefore the Queen has ordered me to strike
Your canopy, and signify to you
That you are a dead woman
Deprived of honour, dignity and queenship.

MARY

God of His Grace called me to be a Queen.
I have been anointed and sacred as a Queen.
I hold my dignity of Him alone
To Him I will resign it, with my soul.
I do not recognize your Queen as mine
Nor her heretical council for my judges.
I will die a Queen, in spite of those whose power
Is like that which the robbers exercise
In some dark den on righteous folk. I trust
That God, after my death, will manifest
The integrity of my cause to all this realm.

Often, Kings in this country have been murdered.
No wonder, then, if I should have that fate
Being of that same royal blood. King Richard
Was treated thus, because of his just rights.

OFFICER (Striking down the canopy)

Madam. There lies your canopy and here
I sit, with covered head. (He sits with covered head.)
                I tell you frankly

END AND BEGINNING

You have no time nor leisure left to you
For idle recreations so be warned.
                    (THE NOBLE ENTERS, *Right Back*)

NOBLE

Madam, God save your grace. You sir, arise
And if you are not brazen, be ashamed
Of such foul rudeness. Since you cannot blush
Means shall be found to make you sensible
Of your brutality. Stand further back.
Madam, I grieve that any officer
Should have behaved thus foully to your grace.
I ask your pardon.
                    I am deeply grieved
To tell you that my Sovereign sends me here
To bring you heavy tidings.
                    Twelve weeks since
We told you of your Doom and sentence passed.

Now we bring warrant to enact that sentence.
I ask that you will hear it read aloud.
First show her Grace the Kingdom's seal affixed.
                    (THE OFFICER *shows the seal*)

MARY

I observe the great seal. I attend the reading.

13

END AND BEGINNING

Read, then, the warrant of our Sovereign Queen.

Elizabeth, by the grace of God, Queen of England, France and Ireland:—knowing the sentence given by Us and others of Our Council against the erstwhile Queen of Scotland, bearing the name of Mary, we now command and enjoin you to take the said Queen of Scotland and see that execution be done upon her person, for which this shall be your full and sufficient discharge forever. From our House at Greenwich, Feb. 1st, the 29th year of our Reign.

I display the Sovereign's signature appended.
God save the Queen.

MARY

In the name of God, these tidings are most welcome.
I bless and praise His Power that the end
Of all my bitter sufferings is at hand.
I did not think the Queen, my sister Queen,
Would ever have consented to my death.
God's will be done.
He is my witness, I shall render up
My Spirit to His Hands all innocent

14

END AND BEGINNING

Of all offence against her.
I shall appear before God's Majesty
Clear of all crimes whereof I am accused.
That soul is far unworthy of the joys
Of Heaven, whose body cannot bear one moment
The executioner's stroke. Death will be welcome.
What time has been appointed for my suffering?

NOBLE

To-morrow morning at eight o'clock, Madam.

MARY

That is very sudden and leaves me no time
For preparation. I have not yet made
My Will, because my papers have been seized
Needs must that I endeavour to provide
For faithful servants who have sacrificed
All things for my sake and in losing me
Will lose all things. I therefore beg of you
A little longer time, to make my will
And fit my soul for death.

OFFICER

                    You have had time.
It's more than two months since I brought you word
You were condemned.

END AND BEGINNING

No, no, madam, alas.
It is not in our power to grant you time.
You die to-morrow at the hour named.
But to prepare your soul, with consolation
You may have either the Bishop or the Dean.
The Dean is a most learned theologian,
Able to show the errors of the falsehood
In which you were brought up, and teach the truth.
And as you have so little time to live
It would be well if you confessed your faults
And seized the true faith for your soul's salvation,
Not trifle with vain toys. You have some wisdom,
And may be able to discern the truth,
Hearing the learned Dean.

MARY

I have heard much,
And read much, on this subject of salvation
Since I was prisoner here. My mind's resolved
To die in the religion of my baptism.
I willingly would give ten thousand lives
If that might be, not only shed my blood
But bear the harshest tortures, in that cause.

OFFICER

Your life would be the death of our religion,

END AND BEGINNING

Your death will save it. Madam, you say true
You die for the religion of your baptism.

Ah, I have never dared self-flattery so
As think that I was worthy such a death;
And I receive it humbly as an earnest
That I am numbered among God's chosen servants.

I have been harshly used here. I am Queen
Of Scotland, the Queen-Dowager of France,
The great grand-daughter of an English King,
Your Queen's most near relation and true heir.
I who was promised friendship have had prison
For nineteen years, through guile of ministers.
Now, by false accusation, I am cast
Illegally, without authority
To perish by the headsman.
                              I take God
To witness on this Testament, that never
Never did I desire, seek, nor favour
The killing of your Queen.

                    Your book is popish
Your oath no worth.

END AND BEGINNING

MARY

        It is my Church's Gospel.
More sacred, as I think, than that you use.
I thank you; but I will not see your priests.
I beg that I may see my almoner.

NOBLE

That is against our law.

OFFICER

        And against conscience.

MARY

Then I must trust God's mercy to excuse
The want of rites such as His holy Church
Declares to be essential before death.
Tell me this: Has the Queen of England sent
An answer to my letter?

NOBLE

        No. No answer.

END AND BEGINNING

Will she allow my body to be taken
By these my servants to be laid in France
By the late King, my husband, at St. Denis
Or by my Mother, the late Queen, at Rheims?

N O B L E

We do not know this.

M A R Y

               Will your Queen return
My papers, and allow my poor true servants
To have the trifling payments I bequeath them?

O F F I C E R

I think, that as your papers cannot pleasure
Her Majesty, they will be all returned
Your little furniture will be departed
As you dispose.

M A R Y

Is my son well?

END AND BEGINNING

NOBLE

Yes, lady.

MARY

How does he take my treatment?

OFFICER

He digests it.
Such are his words.

MARY

Has he, have other princes
Of Christendom made efforts in my cause?

NOBLE

No, madam, none; they will not, neither can.

MARY

My secretaries: are they dead?

END AND BEGINNING

NOBLE

Alive.

MARY

Is Nau alive?

NOBLE

He is, but in close prison.

MARY

Nau is the author of my death; he has
Sacrificed me to save his own life: surely.

NOBLE (*to* OFFICER)

I remit this lady to your hands again.
You will take charge of her till I return.

FIRST WOMAN (*Coming down*)

Sir, I must make a protest, ere you go.
Think of the suddenness of this announcement
The shortness of the time that you allow

END AND BEGINNING

My royal mistress to dispose affairs
Temporal and eternal: the meanest man
Nay, sir, the vilest criminal on earth
Waiting the cart, would have been granted longer
To fit his soul for death. More courtesy
More reverence, should surely be displayed
To a Princess and Queen, and such a Queen.

NOBLE

I have no power to prolong the time.
> (NOBLE *and* OFFICER *go out*, *Right Back*.)
> (MARY *sits Centre*. WOMEN *weep Left*.)

MARY

Leave weeping, now; be doing: time is short.
Did I not say, my children, this would fall?
Blessed be God that it has fallen, and fear
And sorrow are at an end. Weep not. Lament not.
It cannot help; rather rejoice to see
The end of all my troubles and afflictions.
Did you not mark the power of truth? They said
That I was doomed for an attempt to kill
The Queen of England, of which crime you know
That I am innocent. But now this Lord
Lets out the fact, that it is on account
Of my religion. Oh the glorious thought
That I am chosen to die for such a cause.

END AND BEGINNING

Fill now that little drinking-cup with wine.
                    (FIRST WOMAN *fills and brings*)
I drink to you, my faithful follower,
Wishing you happier days in years to come
Than you have known in prison here with me.
May a blessing from my thanks be with you always
Now will you drink to me?
                    (FIRST WOMAN *kneels*)

FIRST WOMAN

O my beloved Queen, for pity, pardon,
Forgive me if I ever failed or pained you.

MARY

Friend, you can never know, never imagine
The joy your faith has given me all these years.
                    (*To the* SECOND WOMAN)
Now let me drink to you, wishing you blessing
And peace and happiness within your home;
All lovely things that you have sacrificed
To be with me, God thank you for it, friend.
Will you pledge me?

SECOND WOMAN

If ever I offended you, or injured,
Forgive me, I beseech you, oh forgive me.

END AND BEGINNING

That I most gladly do, if there be cause
But cannot think there be. I entreat you
If I have ever treated either of you
With harshness or injustice, pardon me.

FIRST WOMAN

You were never never anything but gentle.

SECOND WOMAN

And we, dull clods, ever remiss and grudging.

MARY (*Sits*)

Let me give last commands my faithful servants.
When I am gone, be constant in religion,
Love one another, and, for my sake, cease
Your little quarrels and your jealousies,
And live in Christian amity together
Which will be easier, now that one has gone
Who used to sow dissension in the household.
(*She rises*)
(*To* FIRST WOMAN)
You, gentle friend, go to my almoner
Since I have been forbidden: ask him from me
To recommend such prayers and gospel verses

END AND BEGINNING

As he thinks fittest for me; ask him, too,
To keep in prayer and vigil with and for me
All through to-night: No. I must write this to him.
Come, then, within and I will write to him.
Then I will part the little queenly splendour
Left to me, with my friends: and so be ready
To start uncumbered on my road to God.

   (*They go out Left Back.*)

    Curtain

OFFICER (*Discovered*)

So, not much longer shall I have this charge,
After these years of ceaseless vigilance,
Daylong and nightlong, plot and counterplot,
Alarms and false alarms, and day and night
Wondering whether rescuers would come
Or whether her fine craft would find a means
To write and bribe and compass an escape.
Now she is in the net with no escape,
And the Queen does it: warrant signed and sealed.
The nobles in commission to enforce it.
I have escaped: it has not fallen to me.

And yet, only a few short days ago,
We keepers had a letter from the Court
From Walsingham and Davison together
Saying that Queen Elizabeth has noted
A lack of zeal in us, that all this time
We have not of ourselves found out a way
Of shortening the Scotch Queen's life; that she,
Elizabeth, thought this a lack of love
In us towards her, and a lack of care
Of true religion and the public good;
That she, Elizabeth, took it unkindly
That we, shrinking from keeping of our oaths,
Cast all the burden of the task on her
Who hated, as we know, shedding of blood
Especially the blood of a princess
So near related.

END AND BEGINNING

This, that so greatly troubled her, was sent
For our good judgments, meaning that the hint
So given should be taken and ourselves
Murder this foreign princess, and then doubtless
Be murdered by the law for doing so.
But God be thanked we were not to be caught
By such like hints of murder: now, to-day
Elizabeth will do the deed herself
Mary will die this morning, and to-night
I shall sleep soundly, knowing she is dead.
O me what utter joy: some little trouble
Perhaps in sending off her foreign servants,
Then peace at last.
         All things are now prepared
For her last scene: the scaffold has been built
In the great hall: the block is in its place
All covered decently with cheap black cloth.
A scarlet cushion lies for her to kneel on
To take the stroke: I've had a fire lit
In the great hall: it is such frosty weather.
Let me recount what other things are ready.
The barricade to keep spectators back.
The Sheriff's spears and the Earl Marshal's men
Standing to arms as guards: the courtyards full
Already, of the countrypeople gathered
To cheer when her head falls. A band of music
To play as though a witch were being burned
The tune of 'Jumping Joan.' Horses are ready
To bear the news to London to the Court.
Ay, and the chief clown of the play is ready
All dressed in black and in his mask of black

END AND BEGINNING

The ruffian headsman, Bull, is in his place,
Lolling upon the scaffold railing joking,
With the earls' grooms and footmen, and at times
Supping his brandy, whetting up his axe
And calling "where's this cow that Bull shall tame."
But there:—after the execution has been done
The Earls must dine: I must attend to that . . .
They will need wine, and good . . . I must give
    orders.

       (He goes out, Right Back.)

FIRST WOMAN

Like a fair day, she has been more beautiful
At sunset. When her treasures had been shared
Among us, she began a farewell letter
To the French King, then wrote her will, and then
Commended us, her servants, to his care.
Poor, beautiful great soul she was exhausted
By all this thought.
At her night prayers she bade me read to her
In Scripture, of some Saint who had sinned greatly
"Read of the penitent thief upon the Cross:—
He was a sinner—not so great as I,"
She cried, "O may my blessed Lord, in memory
Of his dear Passion, in my hour of death
Have mercy on me as He had on him."
Then having listened to those blessed words
She laid her down to rest and closed her eyes.
Her beauty was as quiet as in sleep

END AND BEGINNING

I think she never slept, but inly prayed
Sometimes we saw her smile.

After her rest she called us to her, saying
"I have but two hours' life remaining to me.
Dress me for Death as for a festival."
And, being dressed, she said a piteous thing:—
"In my last instant, I shall be incapable
Of thinking of this body. I beseech you
For the dear love of our most blessed Saviour
Do not forsake me as I suffer death
There in the hangman's hands, but cover me."
In some few minutes now that lovely soul
Will be flung forth from life by ruffian hands;
Torn from this place, which, though it has been
 prison
Has still been home; her love has made it home.
There is no help for us: the thing will be.

   (MARY ENTERS *with* SECOND WOMAN. *She*
   bears her will and papers.)

MARY

Women, I have been very blest this morning.
For though my priest has been forbidden me,
I had the holy elements, with leave
From Rome, to offer them myself, ere death.
I am so stayed with angels, I have comfort
In my so soon release from long affliction.
Once, when I was a child, my uncle told me
"That I had all the courage of my race

29

And should know well how to die." He never
    thought
That I should prove his truth in such a death.

But happiness and earthly greatness pass
Witness myself, the Queen of France and Scotland
By birth and marriage, crowned with worldly honour
Brought subject to the executioner,
Though innocent, thank God, of any crime
The crime alleged is but a flimsy pretext
For my destruction.
               I beseech you both
Be present at my death, be witnesses
Of my deportment and my faith. I know
It will be agony to you to watch:
Yet watch: be witnesses: you love me most.

When all is over, you may be permitted
To bear my body into France: I beg you
Stay all together as a family
Till you can do this.
             I will say farewell
To you, with all my thanks. (*She kisses the* FIRST
    WOMAN)
              And now to you
Farewell, and thanks for countless services.

SECOND WOMAN

O my beloved mistress, I beseech you
Forgive me, and forgive my brother, too.

END AND BEGINNING

MARY

Oh, rise. I forgive him and everyone
As I myself now hope to be forgiven.

FIRST WOMAN

O Madam pardon me, if I say this:—
Renée and Gillies beg me to remind you
They are not in your will: they are not greedy
Of gifts, but pray it never may be thought
That they have been unfaithful in their service.

MARY

That never shall be said. What can I leave them?
Renée shall have . . . (*she writes*) and
Gillies shall have that . . . (*writes*)
I thank you for reminding me.

FIRST WOMAN

                    And madam,
Your almoner . . . you have omitted him.

MARY

True, thank you: that will need a little thought.
                    (*She thinks, then writes.*)
There then, I leave the last of my possessions.

31

And now that I have finished with the world
My friends, let us all kneel and pray together
For the last time.

      (*They kneel, facing slightly Left.*)

MARY

O Domine Deus, speravi in Te;
O care me Jesu, nunc libera me.
In dura catena, in misera paena, desidero
Languendo, gemendo et genu flectendo
Adoro, imploro, ut liberes me.

      (*There is a knocking on the door R. Back.*)
See what the knocking is.

      (FIRST WOMAN *goes*)

FIRST WOMAN

Speak, who is there?

OFFICER

Her hour has come: the clock has stricken eight.

FIRST WOMAN

Her Majesty is praying with her servants.

END AND BEGINNING

Ah. Let her pray then for a little while.

MARY

Unbolt the door; there must be no resistance . . .
That would bring violence.
                    (FIRST WOMAN *returns*)
                              Come, sisters, let us pray.
"Thou art my rock and my fortress
Therefore for Thy Name's sake, lead me.

I am forgotten as a dead man.
I am like a broken vessel.

I have heard the slander of many
They devised to take away my life.

Cast me not away from thy presence.
Take not thy holy spirit from me.
            (*There is a knocking at the door*.)
The Lord is my refuge and my fortress
My God, in Him will I trust.
            (*The knocking again*.)
Go, open to them; then return to us.
            (*The* FIRST WOMAN *opens the door*: *then returns
            and kneels*.)
Because thou hast made the Lord thy habitation
There shall no evil befall thee.
            (*The* OFFICER ENTERS *silently*.)

For He shall give his angels charge over thee
To keep thee in all His ways.

They shall bear thee up in their hands."

OFFICER

See. I am come. I am come.

MARY (*To* SECOND WOMAN)

Give me the little cross into my hand.
   (*The* NOBLE ENTERS. MARY *rises.*)

MARY

So, gentlemen, you come to seek for me.
I am ready and am resolute to die.
So let us go. But I am very lame.
Help me, my friends. (*The* WOMEN *help her.*)
   (*They take two or three steps, then stop.*)

FIRST WOMAN

Your Majesty . . . this thing we cannot do.
We'll wait upon you, die with you, if granted
But oh, we cannot lead you to your death.

34

END AND BEGINNING

MARY

You are right. (*To* NOBLE.) See, Sir; my servants
 cannot lead me
To death: I cannot walk without support.
I must have help.

NOBLE

   We will assist you down.

OFFICER

You women, stand aside and come no further.

FIRST WOMAN

But we come, too.

SECOND WOMAN

   We are to go with her.

OFFICER

You'll stay, or you'll be made to, by brute force.
You foreign, Romish hussies: get you back.

35

END AND BEGINNING

FIRST WOMAN

It is most cruel and unparalleled
To rob her at her death of faithful servants
Who have borne many years of prison with her.

OFFICER

Cruel or not, you'll find it is the case.

MARY

I have requests to make: let them be granted . . .
The money given by me to Curle my servant
It has been snatched from him by brutal hands.
May it be restored to him?

OFFICER

Why, yes: it shall be.

MARY

May all my servants be allowed to have
My poor bequests?

NOBLE

Yes, certainly, they shall.

36

END AND BEGINNING

MARY

May they be kindly treated and sent safely
To their own countries after I am dead?

NOBLE

I cannot doubt it: nay, I promise it.

MARY

I thank you deeply for these courtesies.
Lastly, I conjure you, that these poor friends
My dear, afflicted servants may be with me
There at my death, that they may see me die.

NOBLE

No, madam, what you ask cannot be granted.
For if it should be, some of them with speeches
Swoonings and what not, would be grievous to you.
And troublesome and noisome to ourselves
We've had experience of friends at headings.
Also they would not stick
To put some superstitious trumpery in practice
The least would be dipping their handkerchiefs
Into your Grace's blood for relics of you.
It would be most unfit to permit this.

END AND BEGINNING

I will give my word, although it be but dead,
My Lord, that they shall do none of these things.
Alas, poor souls, the only good they ask
Is to take leave of me. I hope your Mistress,
Being a Maiden Queen,
Will vouchsafe, for the sake of Womanhood,
That women may be by me at my death.
I know her Majesty hath not given you
Such strict commission, but that you might grant me
Far greater courtesy than this . . .
Even were I woman of far meaner calling.

OFFICER

What shall it be, Sir? I'm against it, truly.

NOBLE

Madam, the inconveniences are such
As I have told you. These must stand aside.

MARY

I am Cousin to your Queen, of the Blood Royal
Of Henry Tudor, Dowager of France,
And sacred and anointed Queen of Scotland,
Yet you refuse me this.

END AND BEGINNING

NOBLE (*To* OFFICER)

It is harsh measure.
She is a peerless lady.

OFFICER

These are not.
These will but scream and swoon and cause dis-
turbance
And put the headsman off his stroke belike.

NOBLE

There will be guards enough to quiet them.

OFFICER

That, sir, is not the point: they will upset
The dignity and office of the law
And rouse the sympathies of malcontents.

NOBLE

I'll run the risk of that.
(*To the* QUEEN.) Madam, I grant you
Leave to choose two from out your women servants.

END AND BEGINNING

I choose these two: the best loved that I have.

NOBLE

If, as we pass, you would select four men
Out of your household, I will grant you those.

MARY

Let me then choose the four dear faithful ones,
Good Andrew Melville, Master of my Household,
    (*To* SECOND WOMAN)
Will you go bid him meet me at the stairfoot?
Come with him there.

            (SECOND WOMAN *goes out L. Back.*)
And you, will you go call Bourgoigne and Gervais
And Gourion, my doctors, who have tended
Me, in my sicknesses these many years?
Tell them to follow to the Court below.
Let them bring you.

            (FIRST WOMAN *goes out Left Back.*)
                (*To* NOBLE)
Sir, let me thank you truly for this grace . . .
It will mean much to these poor friends of mine.
Now, sir, another kindness if you will,
Lend me your arm to help me down the stairs
When we have reached the level of the hall,

END AND BEGINNING

Then I will walk alone, the few brief steps
That lead me to the presence of my God.

> (*She goes out Right Back, leaning on the*
> NOBLE'S *arm. The* OFFICER *holds the curtain*
> *and follows her.*)
>
> (A SPIRIT OF BEAUTY ENTERS *Left and goes*
> *Centre.*)

THE SPIRIT

I live in Life's intenseness: everywhere
I bring the heavenly salt of being fair

Something of me is in the torted rings
Of the green viper whipped round flapping wings

And in the bird who floats on the wind's stream
Watching the currents crawl in the sea's gleam;

And in the barry reeds, the velvet slink
Of noiseless pads of death coming to drink;

And in the lion-leap on the gazelle
The desert-skimmer broken at the well;

And in the stallion hurtling like the spear,
And in all bright-eyed things wide-eyed from fear;

And in all butterflies whose scarlet glows
On honey trumpets before summer goes.

*   *   *

In the first primrose from the Spring's green blood,
When blackbirds build behind the blackthorn bud.

END AND BEGINNING

And in the Summer when the living green
Calls the red rose for King, the white for Queen;

In Autumn's apples on the leafless branch;
In cornfields that the harvest moon doth blanch;

In Winter's silence of the Earth grown old
With all the forest standing still i' the cold;

All these are mine: and something of me strives
In childhood's memory of other lives

Of firelight in caves, and water falling
And padding were-wolves in the midnight calling.

*　　　*　　　*

I quicken life: the curling of my lip
Gleams in the forefoot of the leaping ship

I laugh in forges where the hammers smite
Red sparks and yellow from the glowing white

I wrestle in all struggles: on all courses
I urge the wheels: I gallop with the horses.

I triumph in all windvanes set as crown
On swaying spires up above the town

I key the arch beneath which Emperors pass
I am the palace that the conqueror has.

END AND BEGINNING

All conquest and all laurel and all prize
Are madness for the brightness of my eyes.

*   *   *

I am that colour and singing in the mind
That make the painter faint, the poet blind.

I am the tower men think of as they build
I am the gold men think of as they gild

I am the city shining like the sun
With power exercised and glory done.

I am the truth to which the seeker strains
I am the living lightning upon brains.

I am the key by which man's mind unlocks
Wisdom from prison, water from all rocks.

*   *   *

I deck the lovely girl, that men may see
Beauty in Time and in Eternity.

I gird the lively lad, that after ages
May have a story blazoned upon pages.

I move among all living things, to bless
The instant that annuls all nothingness,

That only is eternal, the swift thrill
Into the bliss that killing cannot kill.

END AND BEGINNING

And that my lovers find: and this one finds
In treacheries that stun, in grief that blinds,

In agony of longing to be free,
A centre constant in inconstancy.

* * *

So from the shocking second she will pass
Into the quiet that the planet has

In dewy mornings, when the forest lies
Dark, and the dim world slumbers with shut eyes

And yet no colour glows, and owls are gone
And that still lamp the planet is alone

Possessing all the peace, lighting and riding,
The Hope become alive, beauty abiding.

Among that planet's quiet, she'll descry
The wild duck stringing, crying as they fly

And laughing, fly with them, and see the night
Drift into colour, colour into light

And know the nightmare over, that has been
Living on earth a prisoner and a queen.

What then shall follow, shall be what she wrought:
The faith, the hope, the charity of her thought.
(EXIT Left Back.)

END AND BEGINNING

NOBLE (*enters*)

The purpose of our Queen, Elizabeth,
Declared upon her warrant, signed and sealed,
Has been enacted. It is now my duty
To tell you how the woman, Mary Stuart,
Met death some minutes since there in the hall.

Though she was lame, her spirit was too queenly
To falter before peril: she walked proudly
Straight to the scaffold foot, but asked for help
Up the steep steps. Her jailer helped her up
She smiled on him and said "I thank you, sir,
This is the last trouble that I shall give you."

Then sitting in the chair beside the block
She heard the Warrant for her death proclaimed.
She smiled with a sweet smile and crossed herself
And asked that the old priest, her almoner,
Might be permitted there to pray with her.
That was refused. We could not grant her that.
Then Doctor Fletcher, Dean of Peterborough,
Standing outside the scaffold, bending low,
Began to preach at her. She gently checked him
With "Trouble not yourself nor me, for know
That I am settled in the ancient faith
Defending which I mind to spend my blood."

"Madam," the Dean replied, "change your opinion.
Repent you of your former wickedness."

END AND BEGINNING

"Good Mr. Dean," she said, "good Mr. Dean,
Trouble yourself no more about this matter,
I was born in this religion and am resolved
To die in this religion, by God's grace."

We, seeing her resolved in stubbornness,
Said, "Madam, we will pray with Mr. Dean,
For you, that you may have your spirit lightened
With the true knowledge."

     "O my Lords," she said,
"If you will pray with me, even from my heart,
I'll thank you for it: but to pray with you
After your manner,
You being not of the one faith with me,
Would be a sin."

     At this I told the Dean,
"Speak, at your pleasure."

     So the Dean began
Some bitter hometruths against Anti-Christ,
Good comfortable doctrine: a soul's purge:
Alas, she did not heed: like the deaf adder
She turned from him.

     She read aloud some Psalms
And prayed in Latin, then in French and English,
For God's forgiveness of her sins and foes.
For the afflicted Church, and the two kingdoms,
Then for her Son and Queen Elizabeth.

END AND BEGINNING

Then, rising from her knees, she raised her cross
And cried on Christ to take her and blot out
Her sins.

                      At this I interrupted her.
"Madam," I said, "it would be better for you
To eschew such trumpery and bear your Lord
Deep in your heart."

                    She answered a strange thing:
"How can I bear in hand a carven image
Of my Redeemer without bearing Him
Deep in my heart as well?"

The headsmen knelt and begged for her forgiveness.
She said, "I forgive you and all the world
With all my heart, because I hope this death
Will give an end to all my troubles."

                          At this
She raised her hands as though to lift her coif
To be ready for the block. Then both the hangmen
Came up to help her, but she drew away
And asked them not to touch her. "For," she said,
"I have not been accustomed to such pages;
Nor to disrobe before so great a throng."
She beckoned to her women, who with screams
And cryings, were incapable of helping.
"Come, do not weep," she said. "I am most happy
To leave this world: you also should rejoice
To see me dying in a cause so good.

Nay, be ashamed to weep: if you lament thus
I can but send you hence; remember, friends,
That I have promised for you."

               Then very calmly
She as one going to her rest withdrew
The bright pins from her lawn, and lifted off
Her gold pomander, chain and rosary.

And this, the executioner, John Bull,
Snatched from her hands and thrust it in his shoe.
But the tall waiting-woman who was here
Struggled to get it from him: snatching at it
And wrestling with him there.

               The Scottish Queen
Turned gently to the brute and spoke these words:
"Friend, let her have it, she will give you thrice
Its money value"; but the brute replied,
"It is my perquisite and it is mine."

Then she embraced and kissed and blessed her ladies
And drew on crimson sleeves and bade them bind
A handkerchief and Corpus Christi cloth
Over her eyes. She said, "O do not weep,
But pray for me."

               So she was left alone
Kneeling upon the cushion near the block.
In the dead stillness, her clear thrilling voice
Spoke out with rapture: *In te Domine*.

END AND BEGINNING

And bowing down her head upon the block,
She prayed, *In manus tuas, Domine.*

Then, as one hangman gripped her hands, John Bull
Struck clumsily, and held the head aloft,

And cried "God save our Queen Elizabeth."
"So let her enemies perish," cried the Dean.

But only one man there, answered Amen.
All there were moved by the most piteous end
Of the most gracious, courteous royal lady
That ever was betrayed by brutal men
And greedy men, and scoundrels and base knaves,
Falsehood, and savagery and forgery.

Not yet are all the damned indignities
Done on her body that have been commanded:
I will not speak of those, only say this,
That I shall ever bitterly repent
The orders laid upon me to make harsh
Her passing from this world.
No man, not even a courtier, can betray her
Again, forever: as I think, her reign
As Queen, begins now. She is beautiful
In the world's heart, and human policy
Has done its worst upon her and yet failed.
May her lovely spirit be in bliss this moment.

(He goes out.)

49

END AND BEGINNING

(*The Curtain is nearly drawn, and the light dimmed. After ten seconds, the* SPIRIT OF MARY *enters silently to the Centre of the stage.*)

MARY

How soon the bitternesses cease:
This little minute from release,
Has made them end.
In my beginning there is peace.

O marvellous quiet, without fear
Of what can happen or appear
By chance or will.
Life at its very heart is here.

O excellence beyond all trust,
O ecstasy untoucht by dust,
O treasure true,
Untettered by the moth and rust.

I lift in quiet into light,
Exultant, deathless, infinite,
Joy beyond joy.
The beauty equal with the might.

Curtain.